Help Lord, Help!

PROPHETIC AFFIRMATIONS

BARBARA LYONS SLADE

Print information available on the last page.

Rev. date: 03/22/2023

To order additional copies of this book, contact:
Xlibris
844-714-8691
www.Xlibris.com
Orders@Xlibris.com
825230

Contents

In Memory of

Norbert Youngblood,
a man who suffered greatly in his
body but kept his spirit strong by
faithfully speaking the Word over his life.

What Are Prophetic Affirmations?

Prophetic Affirmations are statements you make that correspond with the scriptures. They are words you speak that agree with God's will, His purposes, and His plans.

Benefits of Speaking Prophetic Affirmations

• Speaking Prophetic Affirmations will help you develop God-centered thoughts and encourage an optimistic point of view. Your thoughts, attitude, and beliefs are foundational to how you respond to adversity.

• Speaking Prophetic Affirmations will draw you closer to God, help you acknowledge His presence in your life, and give you a greater revelation of His character. The more you know about God, the easier it will be for you to believe what "He says."

• Speaking Prophetic Affirmations will increase your faith and is a practical discipline for learning how to empower yourself by what you say. As you speak God-approved words, consistently and intentionally, they will renew your mind, reshape your thoughts, and ultimately change your life.

How to Use
"HELP LORD, HELP!"

Each section includes Words of Inspiration, Scriptures, Prophetic Affirmations, Personal Reflections, and Prayers.

1. Begin by reading the **Words of Inspiration**. They will help you to see that you are not alone in your troubles. All Christians suffer, but God, who is the same yesterday, today and forever, is always there to help us.

2. Read the **Scriptures** that are above the Prophetic Affirmations. They are the written Word of God and our instructions for life.

3. Speak the **Prophetic Affirmations** with intent. They will give you hope, deepen your faith, and help you to stay focused on God.

4. Respond to the prompts on the **Personal Reflections** page. This exercise will help you understand the power of words and the impact they have on your daily life.

5. Say the **Daily Prayers** with confidence. Speak to God freely because your Heavenly Father hears your voice and listens to you when you pray.

*The Lord keeps watch over you as you
come and go, both now and forever.
Psalm 121:8 NLT*

Word to the Reader:

I do not know what you are going through, but I do know that you are not alone, and your situation is not without hope. We all experience heartbreak and sorrow, insecurity and fear, unrest and tragedies in this life. Adversities will come, pain is inevitable, and troubles will always haunt us. But we are neither defeated nor hopeless in Christ because God promises to be with us and help us in our time of need.

Therefore, when you find yourself troubled or afraid, remember the one who made you and understands everything about you. God knows your beginning, your end, and everything in between. He is more than able to sustain you in every situation.

Study the Bible. Discover the plans and promises of God, speak the Word over yourself, and make declarations that align with the scriptures. In doing so, you will increase your faith and position yourself to experience the Word of God and the power of God working in you, for you, and through you.

God is everything you need. There is no lack in Him. No matter what life brings, keep rehearsing His promises and watch Him work all things out for your good.

Barbara Lyons Slade

Whatever you dwell on, regarding yourself
or your situation ultimately becomes
"your affirmation."

Renew your mind by what you say.
See yourself from God's perspective.
Say what He says about you.

Help Lord, Help!

Prophetic Affirmations

God created the world.
He made the heavens, the angelic host,
the earth, and all that lives upon it.
He formed the galaxies and set them in place.
He made the sun to govern the day and
told the moon where to set in the evening.
He alone gave birth to the stars and
called each one by name.
He ordained the days and nights
and established both summer and winter.
He determined the height of the mountains
and instructed the oceans how deep to go.
God said, "Let there be," and there was light.
Again, He spoke, and there were birds
in the sky, fish in the seas, and
all sorts of animals filled the land.
He formed man from the dust of the
ground and by His great power breathed
into the man's nostrils the breath of life
and man became a living being.

God created the world.
Surely, we can trust Him with our life.

1.

All Things Are Possible

A righteous man may have many troubles,
but the Lord delivers him from them all.
With God all things are possible.
Psalm 34:19; Matthew 19:26 NIV

Prophetic Affirmations

My problems cannot compare to God's might.
My troubles will always be subject to His power.
God is greater than any adversity.
With God all things are possible.

God can rescue me from all my troubles.
God can sustain me through the hardest of times.
God can free me from every affliction.
With God all things are possible.

God is sovereign over everything that exists.
God is bigger than all my problems.
God can deliver me from every situation.
With God all things are possible.

Rehearse the greatness of God.
Speak about His awesome power.
Declare His promises over your life,
and remind yourself often that
"All things are possible with God."

He will deliver the needy who cry out,
the afflicted who have no one to help.
Psalm 72:12 NIV

Personal Reflection: Write down a breakthrough, a healing, a deliverance, or an answer to a problem you want to see, and then repeat the following words several times, "With God all things are possible."

_____

_____

_____

_____

_____

_____

_____

Daily Prayer

Most High God,
I exalt Your mighty name.

Forgive me, Lord, when I see
my troubles as something I cannot
overcome. Forgive me when I am
distracted by the things of the world
and fail to put my trust in You.

Please help me to see You beyond
my troubles and to acknowledge Your
sovereignty in everything.

You are the God of impossibilities.
You are the God who does great things.
Thank You for Your faithfulness.
Thank You for taking care of me.
In Jesus' name

Before the foundation of the world,
before the stars were set in place,
before the first rain,
before the birds filled the air,
before the flowers bloomed,
before there was day or night,
before you were born,
before you took one breath,
and even before that...

God knew about this season in your
life, and the Lord says to you,
"Be anxious for nothing,
I will take care of you."

2.

Anxious for Nothing

Cast all your anxiety on him,
because he cares for you.
1 Peter 5:7 NIV

Prophetic Affirmations

I cast all my anxiety on God.
I give all my worries to the Lord.
My faith is in God's faithfulness.
I trust God and only God to take care of me.

I cast all my anxiety on God.
I surrender all my concerns to the Lord.
I depend on God to provide for my needs.
I trust God and only God to take care of me.

I cast all my anxiety on God.
I choose to stay calm and rest in God's promises.
I expect God to work all things out for my good.
I trust God and only God to take care of me.

Use your voice to settle your
thoughts, calm your heart,
and renew your mind.

Use your voice to overcome negative
thinking and to free yourself from
feelings of fear, anxiety and worry.

Use your voice to encourage yourself.

Personal Reflection: Is there a situation in your life
that causes you to feel anxious or uneasy? Have you
given it to God?

_____

_____

_____

_____

_____

_____

_____

Daily Prayer

My Lord and my God,
I praise Your victorious name.

I will not drown no matter how difficult
the situation is. I will not lose my mind.
Anxiety will not overcome me.
I will not succumb to stress or despair,
and I will not waiver in faith.

I boldly make these declarations because
You promised, in Your Word, to be with
me in times of trouble, and since You
are with me, I have nothing to fear.

Thank You for always being with me, Lord.
Thank You for Your faithfulness toward me.
In Jesus' name

Sometimes we may find ourselves in a
painfully dark place like facing loss of a
loved one, or property, finances or freedom.
And while we know that life can change in
an instant, unexpected loss of any kind can
provoke feelings of sadness and despair.

As dark and difficult a place like this can be,
believe that God, your Heavenly Father, is
always ready to help. He will be there to
heal your brokenness, comfort you,
strengthen you, and give you
hope for a brighter day.

Rest in the truth that God hears your cries.
He knows the condition of your heart.
He understands your pain and is fully
aware of the troubles you face.

3.

Brokenhearted

*The LORD hears His people when
they call to Him for help. He rescues
them from all their troubles.
Psalm 34:17 NLT*

Prophetic Affirmations

God knows when my heart is broken.
God knows when sorrow has unsettled my soul.
God knows when I feel lost and out of sorts.
I have faith that God will come and rescue me.

God knows when grief has found its way to me.
God knows when tragedy has struck my life.
God knows when I am in a dark place.
I have faith that God will come and rescue me.

God knows when I am sad.
God knows when I am lonely and discouraged.
God knows when I feel wounded and weak.
I have faith that God will come and rescue me.

Speaking Prophetic Affirmations can
be challenging during troubled times.
You may not be in a mood for self-encouragement,
and giving into your pain may seem easier than
trying to overcome your feelings with words.

I pray that you speak the Word regardless of
how you feel, and let the Word work in you.
There is power in what you say.

⁓⥈⥇⁓

Personal Reflection: Choose one of the Prophetic Affirmations from "Brokenhearted" that resonates with your spirit and say it slowly several times. Concentrate on the words as you speak.

_____

_____

_____

_____

_____

_____

_____

Daily Prayer

Father of Mercies,
I praise Your marvelous name.

Lord, You know the depth of my
pain and the seriousness of my situation.
You alone know when I have entered
a dark place, feeling lost and out of sorts.

I believe that You are close to me,
watching me and comforting me,
because You are close to those who
are sad and wounded.

Thank You, God, for strengthening
my soul when I feel weak.
Thank You for healing my broken heart.
Thank You for the compassion You
show to all Your children.
In Jesus' name

What is your response to emotional discomfort?
What do you do when things get tough?
Who do you turn to for encouragement?
What do you do to inspire yourself?

What words do you say to ease your distress?
What words do you speak to console your heart?
Where do you go to lessen your sadness?
What do you do to brighten your soul?

Do you call on God or run to people?
Do you trust the world or put your faith in Jesus?
Who do you turn to for comfort?
Who do you trust with your pain?

4.

Comforted by the Comforter

Praise be to the God and Father of
our Lord Jesus Christ, the Father of
compassion and the God of all comfort,
who comforts us in all our troubles.
2 Corinthians 1:3-4 NIV

Prophetic Affirmations

God comforts me when life is hard.
God comforts me when days are difficult.
God comforts me in times of brokenness.
God comforts me in seasons of sorrow.

God comforts me when I am distressed.
God comforts me when I am discouraged.
God comforts me when I am weary.
God comforts me when I am sad.

God is my comforter.
God is the one who consoles me.
God is the one who shows me compassion.
God is the one who encourages my heart.

God's comfort is rich in mercy
and grace, full of lovingkindness,
and reaches deep within our soul.
We can count on Him to console our heart
and ease our pain because He is the Father
of compassion and the God of all comfort.

Remind yourself of this truth often
and be encouraged by what you say.

Personal Reflection: God is approachable, caring, loving, forgiving, compassionate, merciful, and kind. Write these words down and then speak them until you feel His comforting presence.

Daily Prayer

God of all Comfort and Mercy,
I praise Your gracious name.

Thank You, Lord, for soothing my
soul and carrying my sorrows.
Without You, I feel lost and afraid.
But with You on my side, I live
in hope for a better tomorrow.

Lord, please give me the grace to
endure this season of sadness and the
strength to get through each day.

Thank You for being with me in my suffering.
Thank You for being greater than my pain.
Thank You for being so kind to me.
In Jesus' name

When life becomes burdensome,
and your heart feels so heavy that
giving up seems easier than trying
to find a way out, the world says,
"Hang in there."

When troubles are coming from every
direction, giving rise to desperation
and fear, the world says, "Take a deep
breath; it will all work out."

When your soul is tired, and your
resolve to keep going feels more like
stress and exhaustion, the world says,
"Take care of yourself."

The world may offer sound advice,
but when troubles come our way,
James 1:2 says, "Count it all joy."

5.

Count It All Joy

*Count it all joy when you fall into
various trials, knowing that the testing
of your faith produces patience. But let
patience have its perfect work, so that you
may be perfect and completely developed
[in your faith], lacking in nothing.*
James 1:2-4 NKJV, AMP

Prophetic Affirmations

I count it all joy when my faith is being tested.
I count it all joy when I fall into various trials.
I count it all joy when life starts to get me down.
I count it all joy when troubles come my way.

I count it all joy because the testing
of my faith produces patience.
I count it all joy because the testing of
my faith causes me to mature in Christ.

I count it all joy because the testing of
my faith strengthens my character.
I count it all joy because the testing
of my faith draws me closer to God.

When you speak words that align
with the scriptures, you are speaking
words that agree with God.

When you speak words that agree
with God, you are speaking words that are
true, empowering, and life-changing.

Keep speaking.
There is power is what you say.

❧

Personal Reflection: Complete this sentence:
"I count it all joy when _____ because it
brings me closer to God."

_____

_____

_____

_____

_____

_____

Daily Prayer

Heavenly Father,
I exalt Your excellent name.

Lord, it can be challenging to count it all
joy when I feel sad. But I am learning
that I do not have to hide my sadness, or
pretend to be upbeat to experience joy,
because joy comes from abiding in You.

I will still take pleasure in You, God,
regardless of how I feel. I will still
rejoice in Your goodness no
matter what my situation is.

Thank You for helping me to
remember that as long as I abide
in Jesus, I can experience joy.
Thank You for all that You do for me.
In Jesus' name

Every time we speak the Word of God over our circumstances, we are speaking light into dark places, peace into chaos, hope into hopelessness, and joy into sadness.

As we continually exalt God's Word over our lives, it will increase our faith, help us to see things from God's perspective, and focus on the blessings we receive as children of God.

Trust in the Lord. Believe that He can provide for you, heal you, strengthen you, and restore you. God is sovereign and all things are possible with Him.

6.

David's Song

*David sang this song to the Lord on
the day the Lord rescued him. He sang:
"The Lord is my rock, my fortress, and my
savior; my God is my rock, in whom I find
protection. He is my shield, the power that
saves me, and my place of safety."*
2 Samuel 22:1-3 NLT

Prophetic Affirmations

God is my fortress and my shield.
God is my deliverer and my defense.
God is my savior and my refuge.
God is the power that saves me.

God is my rock where I find protection.
God is my help in times of hardship.
God is the one who rescues me from my enemies.
God is the power that saves me.

God is my shelter and my stronghold.
God is a place where I can hide.
God is my rock, my refuge, and my rescuer.
God is the power that saves me.

Tell yourself often that God
is a way-maker, a miracle worker,
a problem solver, a deliverer,
a fortress, and a shield.

Every day say out loud
"God alone is my help, and He
is the power that saves me!"

> **Personal Reflection:** Write a name for God that speaks
> to your heart. "God is my _____."

_____

_____

_____

_____

_____

_____

Daily Prayer

Holy and Awesome God,
I praise Your holy name.

Lord, thank You for teaching me how to speak words that build me up, keep me encouraged, and strengthen my soul. Please help me to discipline myself continually in this way, so that I may see myself from Your perspective and not from my limited view.

May my faith increase as I speak Your Word over my life. May my thoughts be renewed as I make statements that agree with Your will. May my life bring You glory as I say what You say and empower myself with truth.

May all that I do be pleasing to You. In Jesus' name

What do you do when
everything around you is falling apart:
unexpected expenditures, betrayal,
wayward children, injury, or injustice?

What do you do when every
report brings discouraging news:
wars, pandemics, violence,
loss of life, tragedies?

What do you do when
adversity has found its way to you:
a traumatic accident, a grim medical
diagnosis, a layoff or eviction notice?

What do you do?

7.

Encourage Yourself

*David and his men came to the town, and it was
burned, and their wives and sons and daughters
were taken captive. David was greatly distressed,
for the men spoke of stoning him because the souls of
them all were bitterly grieved. But David encouraged
and strengthened himself in the Lord his God.*
1 Samuel 30:3,6 AMPC

Prophetic Affirmations

I encourage myself in the Lord.
I strengthen myself by reading the Word.
I make myself strong by relying on the scriptures.
I build myself up through prayer and praise.

I encourage myself in the Lord.
I activate my faith by trusting in what God says.
I lift myself up by focusing on God's promises.
I inspire myself by speaking words of victory.

I encourage myself in the Lord.
I encourage myself by trusting in God's faithfulness.
I encourage myself by trusting in God's sovereignty.
I encourage myself by trusting in God.

It matters every time you speak words of faith.
It matters every time you speak words of hope.

It matters every time you speak
words that give you strength.
It matters every time you speak
words that encourage you.

Keep SPEAKING. It matters.

Personal Reflection: Write about a time in your life where it felt like the world was against you and you had nowhere to go but to God.

_____

_____

_____

_____

_____

_____

_____

Daily Prayer

God of Everlasting Hope,
I praise Your majestic name.

Lord, when I think more about
my problems instead of praying about
solutions, please remind me that
You are a way-maker.

When I only see obstacles,
instead of focusing on the victory,
please remind me that You are the one
who causes me to triumph.

When I only feel disappointment
and the weight of adversity seems more
than I can bear, please remind me to
encourage myself in You.

Thank You for Your lovingkindness.
Thank You for caring about me.
In Jesus' name

Many of us struggle with fears and
anxieties brought on by chronic illness,
death of a loved one, a sudden loss of income,
a dwindling marriage, toxic relationships,
rebellious children, or taking care
of elderly parents.

The good news is that God did not give
us a spirit of fear, anxiety, or worry. His spirit
dwelling in us gives us courage, strength, and
determination; and God does not leave us
alone in our struggles. He is always with
us, and He will not fail to help us.

Lean on God and choose to fight
feelings of uneasiness and trepidation
with faith and courage. Trust God in
all things and depend on Him to get
you through every situation.

8.

Faith Over Fear

*For I am the Lord your God who takes
hold of your right hand and says to you,
"Do not fear I will help you."*
Isaiah 41:13 NIV

Prophetic Affirmations

I choose faith over fear.
I choose victory over defeat.
I choose hope over despair.
I choose to believe that God will help me.

I choose peace over anxiousness.
I choose victory over feelings of failure.
I choose joy over discouragement.
I choose to believe that God will help me.

I choose to rest in God and not grow weary.
I choose to pray and not panic.
I choose to triumph over all my troubles.
I choose to believe that God will help me.

Fight feelings of fear with words of faith.
Battle anxious thoughts with words of peace.
Defeat negative thinking with
words of encouragement.
Renew your mind with words of hope.

Repeat words from the scriptures.
Make statements that agree with God.
Change your life by what you say.

Personal Reflection: Fear will paralyze you. Faith will empower you. Which do you choose?

_____

_____

_____

_____

_____

_____

_____

Daily Prayer

Heavenly Father,
I honor Your great name.

Sometimes situations cause us to
feel hurt, confused, and discouraged.
Sometimes we allow these feelings to
overwhelm us, tempting us to walk
in fear and unbelief.

Your Word says in 2 Timothy 1:7 that
"You did not give us a spirit of fear, but of
power and of love and of a sound mind."

Thank You for giving me a sound mind.
Thank You for giving me courage.
Thank You for helping me to
choose faith over fear.
In Jesus' name

"Lord, I need You, please tell me what to do."

"Father God, please speak to me clearly."

"Holy Spirit, help me to recognize Your voice. Help me to hear what You are saying to me."

These are words we may pray to God when we need insight and direction for a pressing situation. Be encouraged because our Heavenly Father knows what is best for us and He is faithful to answer us when we call to Him for help.

9.

God Hears Me

Praise God, who did not ignore my prayer
or withdraw his unfailing love from me.
His eyes watch over those who do right;
his ears are open to their cries for help.
Psalm 34:15; 66:20 NLT

Prophetic Affirmations

God's eyes are upon me.
God sees everything that is happening to me.
God's ears are open to my cry.
God's ears are attentive to my voice.

God knows what is going on in my life.
God knows the challenges that are before me.
God knows the troubles that have come my way.
God knows the difficulties that I must face.

I know that God listens to me when I pray.
I know that God hears me when I call His name.
I wait with expectation to hear what God will say.
I know that God hears me.
I know that God listens to me when I pray.

Prophetic Affirmations are effective
when you speak them aloud,
say them consistently,
repeat them intentionally,
and declare them faithfully.

Say what God says.
Renew your mind by what you hear.
Empower yourself by what you say.

Personal Reflection: Which Prophetic Affirmation
from "God Hears Me" made you feel more confident
that God does hear you when you talk to Him?

_____

_____

_____

_____

_____

_____

Daily Prayer

Heavenly Father,
I praise Your glorious name.

Thank You for the privilege of prayer.
Thank You for the blessing of being
able to communicate with You.

I believe You hear me when I pray,
and although I may not see the
answer right away, I am confident
that You will respond to me.

Thank You for listening to my voice.
Thank You for hearing my heart.
Thank You for answering my prayers.
In Jesus' name

Stay encouraged.
God will work things out for you.

Keep believing.
God will strengthen and uplift you.

Keep hoping.
God will not abandon you.

Be patient.
God will comfort and sustain you.

Have courage.
God will support and empower you.

Have faith.
God has great plans for you.

10.

God Is My Somebody

*Be strong and of good courage; do not
be afraid, nor be dismayed, for the Lord
your God is with you wherever you go.*
Joshua 1:9 NKJV

Prophetic Affirmations

I have somebody that walks beside me.
I have somebody who has my back.
I have somebody that I can count on.
I have somebody who is always with me.

God is my somebody.
When I start to worry, God gives me peace.
When I am disappointed, God gives me hope.
When I feel low, God is there to comfort me.

God is my somebody.
When I feel hurt, God lifts me up.
When I feel defeated, God gives me courage.
When I am weak, God gives me strength.

There is a story to be told even in sorrow.
There is gladness to be shared even in grief.
Your test will always be your testimony
and your problems are a platform
for grateful praise.

Stay encouraged.
Trust in God's faithfulness.
Take comfort in His peace.

Personal Reflection: Write a statement of faith for a situation you recently experienced.

_____

_____

_____

_____

_____

_____

_____

Daily Prayer

Heavenly Father,
I bless Your great name.

God, I call You my "somebody,"
because You are always there.
You never disappoint me, reject me,
or make me feel unworthy.

You are my somebody, God.
You are my comforter, my healer,
my deliverer, and my savior.
You are my fortress and my hiding place.

I can trust You, God.
I can count on You, Father.
Thank You for being my somebody.
Thank You for being my Lord.
In Jesus' name

Hurricanes, high winds, or blistering days
are like troubles that come upon us in rolls
and waves. One moment the sun is shining,
not a cloud in the sky, then tragedy strikes,
tempting us to ask, "God, why?"

The Bible tells us in John 16:33 that
"In this life, we will have sorrow;" if not
today, it may be tomorrow. And unlike
the weather, which some can predict,
adversities show up everywhere, who
can say when or how they will hit?

Hard times come to all of us, and
problems never cease. That is why Jesus
tells us to "Come into His presence and
rest in His peace" (Mark 6:31 NIV).

11.

God Is My Strength

God is our refuge and strength, always
ready to help in times of trouble.
Psalm 46:1 NLT

Prophetic Affirmations

God is my refuge and my strength.
God is always ready to help.
God is a calm place where I can rest.
God is a fortress where I can hide.

God is my refuge and my strength.
God is always ready to help.
God is my anchor when my world gets shaky.
God is my rock when I am afraid.

God is my refuge and my strength.
God is always ready to help.
God saves me when I feel overwhelmed.
God lifts me up when life is hard.

Use your voice to remind yourself
of God's strength and power.

The words you say will encourage your heart.
The words you say will reshape your thoughts.
The words you say will increase your faith.
The words you say will change your life.

Personal Reflection: As you think about the strength of God, complete this statement: "God keeps me strong when_____."

_____

_____

_____

_____

_____

_____

_____

Daily Prayer

God of all Strength and Might,
I exalt Your majestic name.

Lord, please help me to be strong
in You and in Your mighty power.
Help me to trust in Your strength
when I get overwhelmed.
Help me to depend on Your strength
when I get discouraged.
Help me to rest in Your strength
when I get weary.

Lord, thank You for giving me the
strength to face anything with courage
and confidence.

Thank You for being my source of
strength and for making me strong in You.
In Jesus' name

God can mend your heart.
God can strengthen your emotions.
God can restore your mind.
Nothing is too hard for God.

God can heal your body.
God can take away your pain.
God can restore your health.
Nothing is too hard for God.

God can do the impossible.
God can do the unbelievable.
God can do the miraculous.
Nothing is too hard for God.

12.

Healing Is Mine

He has borne our griefs, and He
has carried our sorrows and pain.
By His stripes (wounds) we are healed.
Isaiah 53:4-5 AMP

Prophetic Affirmations

I am the healed of the Lord.
Jesus endured great pain for me.
With the stripes that wounded Jesus
I am healed and made whole.

I am the healed of the Lord.
I am healed of every sickness.
I am healed of every disease.
I am healed of every condition.

I am the healed of the Lord.
Jesus endured great pain for me.
With the stripes that wounded Jesus
I am healed and made whole.

Every time you speak
the Word of God
you are depositing the life
of God and the power of God
in your spirit, in your soul,
and over your circumstances.

Keep speaking.
Increase your faith by what you hear.
Change your life by what you say!

Personal Reflection: Fill in the blank. "I believe God desires to heal me of_____." Repeat the words often until you believe what you say.

Daily Prayer

God of Miracles,
I praise Your excellent name.

It was a miracle that You sent Jesus
to die for me so that I could live with
You forever. It was a miracle that Jesus
took my sins, my sicknesses, and my
diseases upon Himself. It was a miracle
that Jesus gave His life for me.

Lord, may I experience a miracle in my
body as You minister Your healing power
in me. May I come to know you personally
as "The Lord who heals and the one
who causes me to recover."
In Jesus' name

We encounter many afflictions and
adversities in this life, and although they
may differ in degree, we all experience
similar emotions, such as fear, grief,
anxiety, disappointment, anger,
frustration, pain, and sorrow.

But thanks be to God who not only
understands our emotions but
addresses them in the Word.

I encourage you to read the Bible.
Find something appropriate for your
situation and speak those scriptures over
yourself. Doing this consistently will
equip you with words of power that will
rise in your spirit when you need them most.

13.

I Can Make It

Whatever I have, wherever I am,
I can make it through anything in the
One who makes me who I am.
Philippians 4:13 MSG

Prophetic Affirmations

I can make it when I am weak
and tired because God will strengthen me.
I can make it when I am sad and
troubled because God will rescue me.

I can make it when I feel hopeless
and scared because God will encourage me.
I can make it when I am shattered
and broken because God will comfort me.

I can make it when I am lost and lonely
because God is always beside me.
I can make it no matter what life brings
because God will take care of me.

You will receive encouragement and
strength when you speak words that
align with the scriptures.

You will experience peace and
comfort when you speak words
that agree with God.

Keep speaking faith-filled words.
Keep inspiring yourself by what you say.

❧

Personal Reflection: Which Prophetic Affirmation
from "I Can Make It" helped most with a struggle you
are facing in your life?

_____

_____

_____

_____

_____

_____

_____

Daily Prayer

Most Holy God,
I bless Your great name.

Forgive me for the times that I have
neglected Your Word and found myself
dwelling on things that caused me to
be fearful and unproductive, even to
the point of believing the lie that
I cannot make it.

Help my unbelief, Lord, and give
me the courage to do all that You
have purposed for my life.

Please help me to stay focused on You
and to gain strength from Your Word.
Thank You for Your faithfulness.
In Jesus' name

No matter what you feel,
no matter how deep the pain,
no matter how sad the heart,
let it be well with your soul.

No matter how great the loss,
no matter how confusing the situation,
no matter how bleak things may seem,
let it be well with your soul.

No matter how depressing the day,
no matter how somber the hour,
no matter what your life holds,
let it be well with your soul.

14.

It Is Well With My Soul

Why, my soul, are you downcast?
Put your hope in God, for I will yet
praise him, my Savior and my God.
Psalm 42:5 NIV

Prophetic Affirmations

It is well with my soul
even when things look dim.
It is well with my soul even when
I feel lonely and discouraged.

It is well with my soul even
when I am tired and overwhelmed.
It is well with my soul even when
I feel like I cannot make it another day.

It is well with my soul because I believe God.
It is well with my soul because my faith is in God.
It is well with my soul because I trust God.
It is well with my soul because my hope is in God.

God's words are full of power.
God's words are true and reliable.
God's words are alive and active.
God's words are eternal.

Let His words stay on your lips.
Speak them consistently.
Be encouraged by what you say,
and let it be well with your soul!

***

Personal Reflection: Close your eyes and say the words "It is well with my soul." Keep repeating these words until you feel the presence of God within you.

_____

_____

_____

_____

_____

_____

_____

Daily Prayer

God of Salvation and Hope,
I exalt Your glorious name.

Your Word tells me that "The troubles
I now face are temporary and small
compared to what You have planned for
those who belong to You. For the things
I see now will soon be gone, but the
things I cannot see will last forever"
(2 Corinthians 4:17-18).

Thank You that my troubles are temporary.
Thank You that my life is secure in Jesus.

May the glory of Your peace be upon me.
May Your grace and mercy follow me always.
In Jesus' name

No matter what you go through,
today, tomorrow, next week, next month,
this year or the next, regardless of how
difficult it is or how long it lasts, trust
that God is with you, and He will
not allow your troubles to
be more than you can bear.

He will be there to meet your need.
He will be there to strengthen you.
He will be there to help you rise
above your troubles.
He will be there to save you.

15.

I Will Not Drown

*When you go through deep waters, I will be
with you. When you go through rivers of
difficulty, you will not drown. When you walk
through the fire of oppression, you will not be
burned up; the flames will not consume you.*
Isaiah 43:1-3 NLT

Prophetic Affirmations

God is with me when I go through troubled times.
God is with me when I go through deep waters.
God is with me when I am lonely and afraid.
God is my deliverer; I trust Him to save me.

God is with me when adversity is at my doorstep.
God is with me when sorrow has come my way.
God is with me when life seems harsh and unjust.
God is my deliverer; I trust Him to save me.

God is with me when pain wants to consume my body.
God is with me when life seems too much to bear.
God is with me when bad news just keeps coming.
God is my deliverer; I trust Him to save me.

God will help me because He loves me.
God will help me because I am His child.
God will help me because He is faithful.
God will help me because He is God.

Repeat the statements above.
Speak them until the words refresh your spirit.
Speak them until the words strengthen your heart.
Speak them until you believe what you say.

Personal Reflection: Complete this statement: "God is with me and He will deliver me from _____."

Daily Prayer

Faithful God,
I bless Your powerful name.

Lord, You know everything about my life.
You know every challenge I will face,
every hardship, every season of sadness,
every moment of discouragement and
every feeling of fear.

Thank You that no matter how hard
life gets, You will not let me drown.
You will be there to encourage me.
You will be there to uphold me.

You are my deliverer and the
power that saves me.
In You only do I put my trust.
In Jesus' name

When we go through tough situations
we may not feel joyful. On the contrary,
we may feel shattered and broken as if
sadness would consume our souls.

Nevertheless, God promised in His Word
to give us joy, and He desires that we
allow His joy to be a source of strength in
times of adversity. Our situation may not
change, the outcome may not be as we
like, but the promise of joy still belongs
to those who are His.

16.

Joy Comes in the Morning

*I trust God with all my heart. He helps
me, and my heart is filled with joy. Each
day He carries us in His arms, and when
doubts fill our minds, His comfort gives
us renewed hope and cheer.
Psalm 28:7; 68:19; 94:19 NLT*

Prophetic Affirmations

God fills my heart with joy.
God encourages my soul.
God carries me in His arms.
My Father wraps me in His joy.

God fills my heart with joy.
God strengthens me when I am sad.
God consoles me when I feel overwhelmed.
God comforts me when I am hurting.

God fills my heart with joy.
God gives me faith for a brighter day.
God's Word gives me renewed hope.
God's promises give me joy.

Press through hard times by speaking
the promises of God over your life.

Speak of His joy and be joyful.
Speak of His comfort and be comforted.
Speak of His power and be at peace.

Use your voice to encourage yourself.

Personal Reflection: The words you speak have
tremendous power. They can build you up or tear you
down. They can lift your spirit or cause you to sink
in despair. What words will you speak over your life
today?

Daily Prayer

Heavenly Father,
I praise Your righteous name.

Lord, I want to feel joyful but there are
times when I feel so empty inside it
is hard even to smile.

Please help me to remember that the joy
You give is not based on circumstances,
but the gladness of heart that comes
from knowing and abiding in You.

Please help me to find happiness in the
small things, to be grateful for everything,
and to recognize that joy is a choice.

As I surrender myself to You, Father,
may Your joy rise mightily in me.
In Jesus' name

The challenges we face are not a surprise
to God. When He created the world,
He knew we would encounter hardships
that would weigh us down and cause us to
feel heavy-hearted, weak, and uninspired.

He knew that terrible offenses and violations
of every sort would tempt us to respond in
fear and panic, and when emotional pains
would cut so deep that moving forward
would seem almost impossible.

That is why our Heavenly Father
beckons us to trust Him in our troubles
and to put our faith in Him. He is a great
God, who is more than able to deliver us,
rescue us, strengthen us, and restore us.

17.

Keep Hope Alive

We have troubles all around us, but we are not defeated. We do not know what to do, but we do not give up the hope of living. We are hurt sometimes, but we are not destroyed.
2 Corinthians 4:8-9 NCV

Prophetic Affirmations

I will rise above my troubles.
I will work through every obstacle.
I believe I can do all things in Christ.
God is my hope; my trust is in Him.

I will hold on to God's promises.
I will strengthen myself in God's Word.
I believe I can do all things in Christ.
God is my hope; my trust is in Him.

I live with expectation to see a better day.
I look forward to what God has planned for me.
I believe I can do all things in Christ.
God is my hope; my trust is in Him.

Remind yourself every day that God is
your hope, your rock, and your support.
He is always with you. He will never
abandon you or fail you.
"He recognizes and welcomes anyone
looking for help, no matter how desperate
the trouble" (Nahum 1:7 MSG).

Rehearse the faithfulness of God.
The Lord will honor what you say.

Personal Reflection: In your own words, create a
Prophetic Affirmation that will inspire a day of hope
and encouragement.

_____

_____

_____

_____

_____

_____

_____

Daily Prayer

Trustworthy and Faithful God,
I honor Your awesome name.

Lord, I believe that I can do all things
in Christ. I believe that I can endure
temptation, withstand the enemy's attacks,
and gain victory in every battle.
I believe it because You said it.

I believe that my best days are ahead of
me and that Your plans for me are good.
I believe it because You said it.

Now, Lord, when troubles come my way,
and life gets too big, may I not waiver in
faith, but draw near to You, and
anchor myself in what "You say."
In Jesus' name

Lord, Help!
These are words we call out to God when
we are hurting and in despair, when the
burden seems too heavy to carry, or when no
other words seem appropriate.

Lord, Help!
These are words that reach the ears of God,
appealing to His compassion, mercy, and
grace; words that break forth into heaven
imploring God to act in our behalf.

18.

Lord, Help!

Some wandered in the wilderness, lost and homeless. Some sat in darkness and deepest gloom. They rebelled against the words of God; they fell, and no one was there to help them. "LORD, help!" they cried, and He saved them from their distress.
Psalm 107:4-6; 10-13 NLT

Prophetic Affirmations

God knows my desperate cry.
God hears me when I call to Him.
God saves me from distress and darkness.
I trust God to come and rescue me.

God knows when my heart is heavy.
God knows when I am in pain.
God knows when I am in deep trouble.
I trust God to come and rescue me.

God knows when I have wandered from His path.
God knows when I do not know which way to turn.
God knows when I have lost myself in worldly pursuits.
When I cry, "Lord, Help," God comes to rescue me.

Acknowledge God's presence in your
life by speaking about His blessings,
talking about His plans,
declaring His promises, and
affirming yourself in His Word.

Use your voice to remind yourself that
God is a ready help in trouble.
Use your voice to remind yourself
to always acknowledge God.

Personal Reflection: Write down a time that God
rescued you. Believe that He will do it again.

_____

_____

_____

_____

_____

_____

Daily Prayer

God of Divine Deliverance,
I praise Your mighty name.

Lord, please forgive me when I have
lived unwisely and caused myself to have
problems that I could have avoided.
I repent for making decisions that
work against my good.

Thank You for delivering me from trouble.
Thank You for delivering me from bad decisions.
Thank You for delivering me from myself.

You are the Lord, my helper.
You are the God I trust.
In Jesus' name

Life is unpredictable.
We do not know what the day,
even the moment, will bring.
A devasting call, a disaster that strikes
without warning, or any unexpected
change can cause anxiety or fear.

Rest assured because God never changes.
He is our rock and a place of safety.
He is eternally faithful and perfect in all
His ways. His mercies never cease, and
His lovingkindness is for a lifetime.

Whether it is a small glitch in our day,
or a tragedy that shocks our soul,
may we remember to thank God for
His many blessings and His promise
to help us in our time of need.

19.

My Forever Praise

*May I never forget the good things God
does for me. He forgives all my sins and
heals all my diseases. He redeems me from
death and crowns me with love and tender
mercies. He fills my life with good things.*
Psalm 103:2-5 NLT

Prophetic Affirmations

God forgives all my sins.
God heals all my diseases.
God gives me renewed strength.
I will forever praise God for His goodness.

God redeems me from troubles and affliction.
God crowns me with love and tender mercies.
God fills my life with good things.
I will forever praise God for His goodness.

I praise God for His daily benefits.
I praise God for His lovingkindness.
I praise God for all He does for me.
I will forever praise God for His goodness.

Let the words you speak bring you peace.
Let the words you speak fill you with joy.
Let the words you speak strengthen your soul.
Let the words you speak be worthy of praise.

Let the words you speak bring honor to God.
Let the words you speak give Him continual glory.
Let the words you speak exalt God's name.
Let the words you speak be worthy of praise.

Personal Reflection: God's blessings are endless. Write a note to Him describing what He has done for you today.

_____

_____

_____

_____

_____

_____

Daily Prayer

Awesome and Amazing God,
I praise Your excellent name.

Thank You for being my companion
and my comforter; how thankful I am.
Thank You for being my deliverer,
my friend, and the one who
defends me; how encouraged I am.

Thank You for being my healer and
my helper; how grateful I am.
Thank You for being my provider,
my protector, and the one who
saves me; how comforted I am.

Thank You, Heavenly Father, for
being everything that I need.
How blessed I am.
In Jesus' name

Sometimes it feels like no one understands the gravity of our pain or the emptiness we feel in our hearts. And if we let these feelings linger, they can lead to isolation, discouragement, and despair.

In these times of loneliness, we must choose not to fall into self-pity or believe the lies of the enemy that we suffer alone. On the contrary, we must choose to trust God, who is always with us. He knows what we are going through and how we feel at every moment.

20.

Never Alone

O Lord, You know everything about me.
You know everything I do. You go before
me and follow me. You place your
hand of blessing on my head.
Psalm 139:1-5 NLT

Prophetic Affirmations

God knows everything about me.
God knows when my heart is heavy.
God knows when my body is aching.
God knows when my emotions are unstable.
I am never alone.

God knows when I am discouraged.
God knows when I am afraid.
God knows my deepest thoughts.
I am never alone.

God knows everything about me.
God goes before me and follows me.
God's hand of blessing is on my head.
I am never alone.

Keep putting words of truth in your spirit and
continually tell yourself that you are not alone.
In this way, when the enemy comes to tempt
you with thoughts of self-pity and negativity,
you will not fall into his trap.

Over and over rehearse these words:
"I am never alone. God is always with me."
Be encouraged by what you hear.

Personal Reflection: Has there ever been a time when
you felt close to God and something happened to cause
your faith to dwindle? Looking back, can you see how
God was right there with you?

_____

_____

_____

_____

_____

_____

_____

Daily Prayer

Father of all Compassion,
I praise Your holy name.

God, what should I do when I feel alone?
What should I do, Lord, when I feel
as if no one cares?

Please fill me with Your peace, God,
and help me to get out of this place
of self-pity. Give me the courage to
embrace Your love and the strength
to stand on Your promises.

Thank You for never leaving me or
abandoning me. Thank You for
always being there for me.
In Jesus' name

You are not alone in your plight.
There are millions in the same fight.
Stressed out, weary, unsure of the unknown,
holding on to God to help them stand strong.

Hardships and sorrow come to us all.
They may shake us up, but God will not let us fall.
The Lord is always there to show us a way out,
but it must be His way, not our chosen route.

If you want to endure, do it God's way.
He is faithful to help you get through each day.
Whatever you need, God will provide for you.
Pray, watch and wait, and see what He will do.

21.

No Temptation Too Great

*The temptations in your life are no
different from what others experience.
And God is faithful. He will not allow the
temptation to be more than you can stand.
When you are tempted, he will show you a
way out so that you can endure.*
1 Corinthians 10:13 NLT

Prophetic Affirmations

No temptation is too great.
God always provides a way out.
God makes me victorious in Him.
God enables me to stand strong.

No temptation is too great.
God gives me courage to rise above my struggles.
God gives me grace to persevere in every situation.
God enables me to stand strong.

No temptation is too great.
No temptation is more than I can stand.
God is faithful to help me endure.
God enables me to stand strong.

Fight your thoughts
with the Word of God.
Tackle every problem
with the right mindset.

Overcome negative thinking by
speaking God-approved words.
Win the battle in your mind
by what YOU SAY!

⁓⁓⁓

Personal Reflection: Whatever you are facing, God
will help you to overcome it. Complete this statement
of faith. "God is greater than _____."

_____

_____

_____

_____

_____

_____

Daily Prayer

Heavenly Father,
I bless Your wonderful name.

Thank You for providing a way out
of every temptation, even the temptation
to worry, to be fearful, angry or anxious.

Thank You for helping me to stay
focused, to remain calm, and to trust
that You will give me everything
I need to get through each day.
I believe that I can do all things
with You on my side.

Thank You for Your faithfulness,
Your goodness, and Your kindness.
In Jesus' name

God knows when we are hurting.
He knows when we are downcast and
discouraged. He knows when too many
disappointments have invaded our lives,
and the constant letdown begins to
affect our well-being.

Our Heavenly Father knows when
the spirit of depression is waiting at our
door and thoughts of defeat begin to tear
at our souls. He knows, He understands,
and He promises to be with us in troubled
times, gird us with strength, and give
us renewed hope.

22.

Not Without Hope

Is anything too hard for the Lord?
With God all things are possible.
Genesis 18:14; Mark 10:27 NKJV

Prophetic Affirmations

My condition is not hopeless.
My circumstances are not beyond help.
My situation is not too far gone to change.
Nothing is too hard for God.

God is bigger than any affliction.
God is more powerful than any crisis.
God is mightier than any tragedy.
Nothing is too hard for God.

My condition is not hopeless.
My circumstances are not beyond help.
My situation is not too far gone to change.
Nothing is too hard for God.

God is an ever-present help.
He is your hiding place.
He is a shelter from the storm and
a light when things seem dark.
He is your provider and your protector.
He is the one who walks beside you.
He is the one who saves you!

Faithfully remind yourself of who God is,
and then rest in what you say.

Personal Reflection: Write your own Prophetic Affirmation about "Hope."

_____

_____

_____

_____

_____

_____

_____

Daily Prayer

Most Holy God,
I exalt Your great name.

Lord, You know when my heart is
hurting, when my emotions are shaky,
and when my soul aches for the release
of those things that disturb my peace.

You alone can restore my stability,
heal my body, strengthen my mind,
and enable me to withstand the
testing of hardships and afflictions.

Thank You, God, for healing the
brokenness in me, keeping my heart
at ease, and making me feel secure.

To You alone, I surrender my soul.
In Jesus' name

Peace is not the absence of conflict,
discouragement or disappointment.
It does not eliminate feelings of sorrow,
nor guarantee a pain-free life.
It does not mean we will escape
hardship, or never experience feelings
of hopelessness or fear.

Peace is the presence of Jesus.
When we accept Christ in our hearts,
His peace becomes available to us
because He dwells in us; and unlike
what the world offers, the peace of
Jesus is a gift from God that
surpasses human understanding.

Reap the benefit of God's peace by
acknowledging His presence in every
circumstance and let His peace comfort
your soul regardless of what is
happening in your life.

23.

Perfect Peace

*Pray about everything; tell God your needs
and don't forget to thank him for his answers.
If you do this, you will experience God's
peace, which is far more wonderful than
the human mind can understand.*
Philippians 4:6-7 TLB

Prophetic Affirmations

I pray about everything.
I tell God my needs.
I thank God for His answers.
I experience God's perfect peace.

I receive the peace that surpasses understanding.
I receive the peace that comes from God.
God's peace will keep my thoughts on Jesus.
God's peace will keep my soul at rest.

I pray about everything.
I tell God my needs.
I thank God for His answers.
I receive God's perfect peace.

Resist anxious thoughts.

Reject negative thinking.

Refrain from worrying.

INSTEAD

Speak words that strengthen your mind.

Speak words that quiet your spirit.

Speak words that agree with God.

Speak words of peace.

Personal Reflection: Speak the words "I receive the peace of God" over and over. Take a deep breath each time you say the words. How did it feel?

Daily Prayer

Heavenly Father, Lifter of my Soul,
I praise Your holy name.

Lord, when times are hard and troubles
seem to be coming from every direction,
please help me to embrace Your peace;
peace that surpasses human understanding,
peace that will keep my soul at rest.

When my thoughts are blurred,
please bless me with Your peace.
When my heart is heavy,
please bless me with Your peace.
When I feel unsettled and afraid,
please bless me with Your peace.

Thank You for Your perfect peace.
Thank You for caring about me.
In Jesus' name

Are you exhausted, worn-out, bone-tired;
tired when you wake up, tired when
you go to bed, tired of thinking, tired
of having problems, tired of people,
tired of life – just TIRED?

What is the answer, Lord?

Come to me, all who are tired
from carrying heavy loads,
and I will give you rest.
Matthew 11:28 GW

24.

Psalm 23

Because the Lord is my Shepherd,
I have everything I need!
Psalm 23:1 TLB

Prophetic Affirmations

I find rest in Jesus when I am tired.
I find safety in Jesus when I feel overwhelmed.
I find peace in Jesus when I need a quiet place.
Whatever I need, I find in Jesus.

I find hope in Jesus when I am discouraged.
I find comfort in Jesus when I am sad.
I find power in Jesus when I feel depleted.
Whatever I need, I find in Jesus.

I find strength in Jesus when I am weak.
I find joy in Jesus when my spirit is low.
I find help in Jesus when I am troubled.
Whatever I need, I find in Jesus.

Create an atmosphere for change
by the words you speak.

Develop a new way of thinking by
the words of your mouth.

Make a difference in your life
by what YOU SAY.

Personal Reflection: Which Prophetic Affirmation
from "Psalm 23" fits best for how you feel today?

_____

_____

_____

_____

_____

_____

Daily Prayer

Father of the Lord Jesus Christ,
I praise Your holy name.

Thank You for giving me the courage to
walk away from people and situations
that cause me to feel stressed.

Thank You for giving me strength when
I find myself discouraged and exhausted.
Thank You for being my resting place.

No one compares to You, Lord.
No one can do what You do.
No one can meet my needs like You.
Thank You for everything.
In Jesus' name

A thankful heart carries great power.
So let your time of praise become your finest hour.
Begin your day with a right attitude.
Perceiving all things with thanks and gratitude.

Expect the Lord to give you His best.
Impartations of strength, hope, joy, peace and rest.
Remember that God knows what you need.
And He is the one who does amazing deeds.

Think of God's goodness and all He does for you.
Keep your mind focused on Him and what He will do.

25.

Thank God for Everything

*God remembers us in our weakness. He
does not ignore the cries of those who suffer.
He takes care of everyone in time of need.
Psalms 9:12; 136:23 NLT, MSG*

Prophetic Affirmations

I thank God for taking care of my needs.
I thank God for His concern for my life.
I thank God for helping me through difficult times.
I thank God for everything He does for me.

I thank God for being with me in my darkest hour.
I thank God for listening to the petitions of my heart.
I thank God for remembering every tear that I cry.
I thank God for everything He does for me.

I thank God for the hope of a better tomorrow.
I thank God for the promise of a brighter day.
I thank God for His mercies and His lovingkindness.
I thank God for everything He does for me.

The more you speak words of
thanksgiving, the easier it becomes.

The more you speak words of gratitude,
the more grateful you will be.

Keep speaking about God's goodness.
Keep praising God for the things He does.
Keep strengthening yourself by what you say.

Personal Reflection: Write a statement of thanksgiving
to speak over your day. Repeat it over and over.

_____

_____

_____

_____

_____

_____

_____

Daily Prayer

Faithful and True God,
I bless Your great name.

As I humbly come before You, Lord,
I acknowledge that You are a mighty
God, perfect in all Your ways.
You do all things well and are faithful
to work all things out for my good.
May I remember to appreciate the
blessings in my life and the mercies
that You show me each day.

1 Thessalonians 5:18 says,
"No matter what happens, always be
thankful, for this is God's will for you
who belong to Christ Jesus."

I choose to walk in Your will, Father.
I choose to be thankful no
matter what happens.
In Jesus' name

God is the First and the Last,
the Alpha and the Omega,
the Beginning and the End.
He always was and He always will be.

God is all-knowing and all-powerful.
God is sovereign and He is mighty.
God is before all and above all.
He always was and He always will be.

God will be there at the start of your difficulties.
God will be there during times of testing.
God will be there amid suffering and pain.
He always was and He always will be.

26.

The Lord Is There

Those who know Your name will put their
trust in You. For You, Lord, have not
forsaken those who seek You.
Psalm 9:10 NKJV

Prophetic Affirmations

I seek God at the beginning of my troubles.
I go to God because He is my helper.
I trust God in the worst of times.
My soul is at rest because God is always there.

God is greater than any problem.
I can count on God in the midst of every storm.
I choose to believe God beyond my difficulties.
My soul is at rest because God is always there.

I exalt God above bad news and disappointment.
I sing praises to God before the test is over.
My heart is grateful because God alone is my refuge.
My soul is at rest because God is always there.

Speak words that help you to
focus on the greatness of God.

Speak words to help you remember
that nothing is too hard for God.

Speak words to remind yourself
that the Lord is always there.

Personal Reflection: If there is anything troubling you,
write it down and finish it with these words:
"But my soul is at rest because God is always there."

_____

_____

_____

_____

_____

_____

Daily Prayer

Holy and True God,
I honor Your holy name.

When the days are long and
the nights seem even longer,
I know You are there.

When no one sees my tears,
especially the ones I cry at night,
I know You are there.

When pain has no mercy and
comfort is nowhere in sight,
I know You are there.

Thank You for never leaving me, Lord.
Thank You for being my constant companion.
May Your presence be with me always.
In Jesus' name

Today is not a surprise to God.
He knew where you would be,
how you would feel, and what you
would be doing right now.

God knew that the struggles of this world,
the temptations of life, and the testing
of your faith would have you seeking a
change, a transformation, even a miracle.

God knew this day would come and
has already set in motion a season of
healing, refreshing, and restoration.

27.

This Too Shall Pass

*There is a time for everything, and a season
for every activity under heaven: a time to kill
and a time to heal... a time to weep and a
time to laugh, a time to mourn and a time to
dance... a time to tear and a time to mend.*
Ecclesiastes 3:1-7 NIV

Prophetic Affirmations

After a while this too shall pass.
This season of struggling will one day be gone.
This pain I feel now will only be a memory.
The troubles I face today will be a thing of the past.

The time has come for restoration of health.
The time has come for healed emotions.
The time has come to mend relationships.
The time has come to right the wrong.

After a while this too shall pass.
After a while my days will be brighter.
After a while this testing will be over.
After a while this season will end.

Reshape your mind by what YOU SAY!

Speak faith-filled words.
Speak words that are God-approved.
Speak words that align with the scriptures.
Speak words to oppose negative thinking.
Speak words to strengthen your faith.
Speak words to inspire yourself.

Personal Reflection: What are you believing God for?
Keep speaking about it until it happens.

_____

_____

_____

_____

_____

_____

_____

Daily Prayer

God of all Mercies and Grace,
I praise Your glorious name.

Heavenly Father, I lay every negative
emotion on the altar of Your love and
tender mercies. May I find ease from
the troubles of yesterday as I surrender
my past and my pain to You.

I come to You, Father, because You
are the one who can restore my joy.
You are the one who can heal my heart.
You are the one who can bring light
into the dark places of my soul.

I come to You, Father, because I
have no place else to go.
I come to You because You are God.
In Jesus' name

Trust God.
He is the great God above all gods.
He is the one who gives us peace.
He is the one who keeps us safe.
He is the one who has all power.
He is the one who will be with us
in our darkest hour.

Trust God.
He is the Lord God Almighty.
He is the one who gives us hope.
He is the one who gives us courage.
He is the one who makes us bold.
He is the one who will protect us
and comfort us when the
world seems so cold.

Trust God.
He is everything we need!

28.

Trust God

The LORD is my light and my salvation;
so why should I be afraid? The LORD is
my fortress, protecting me from danger,
so why should I tremble?
Psalm 27:1 NLT

Prophetic Affirmations

God is my light and my salvation.
God is my rock and my fortress.
God is my refuge and my protection.
God is my strength; my trust is in Him.

God is my light and my salvation.
God is my shield and my shelter.
God is my hope and my hiding place.
God is my strength; my trust is in Him.

God is my light and my salvation.
God is my comforter and my peace.
God is my help and my healer.
God is my strength; my trust is in Him.

God is trustworthy.
Say those words out loud.
God is faithful.
Say those words with confidence.
God is my hope.
Say those words with expectation.
God is my deliverer.
Say those words with boldness.

Say them all again.
Repeat them until you believe what you say!

Personal Reflection: Complete this sentence:
"God is my strength; I trust Him to _____."

Daily Prayer

Heavenly Father,
I bless Your holy name.

You were there while I was
being formed in my mother's womb.
You knew from the beginning how each
day of my life would unfold.

I trust You, Lord, to help me
live peaceably and productively.
I trust You to help me navigate
through the ups and downs of life.
Without You, I will grow weak
and want to give up; but with You
on my side, I know I can make it.

I trust You because You created me.
I trust You because You are God.
In Jesus' name

Do you ever ask God questions like,
"When are Your promises going to manifest
in my life, what is the answer to my problem,
when am I going to feel better, or when
are things going to change?

Even though we want to see immediate
breakthrough and deliverance, adversities
give our faith a chance to grow. Faith matures
when we have no other place to turn but to God.
Faith is our lifeline when the news is doom
and gloom. Faith is our anchor in the face of
tragedy and our rock during times of testing.

In times, when it feels like your faith
is wavering, remember that faith is not
contingent on the outcome of the situation.
Faith is not measured by what you feel.
Faith exalts God in trouble.
Faith sees God beyond the problem.
Faith believes God, no matter what.

29.

Walk by Faith

For we walk by faith, not by sight.
For without faith it is impossible to
please Him, for he who comes to God
must believe that He is, and that He is a
rewarder of those who diligently seek Him.
2 Corinthians 5:7; Hebrews 11:6 NKJV

Prophetic Affirmations

I walk by faith and not by sight.
I keep my eyes on the promises of God.
I focus on what the Lord says.
I meditate on the scriptures.

I walk by faith and not by sight.
I trust in God's lovingkindness.
I trust in God's mercy and grace.
I trust in God's strength and power.

I believe that God exists.
I believe God rewards those who seek Him.
I believe God is all that He says that He is.
I walk by faith and not by sight.

*What is faith? It is the confident
assurance that something we want is
going to happen. It is the certainty that
what we hope for is waiting for us, even
though we cannot see it up ahead.*
Hebrews 11:1 TLB

Keep talking about what you hope for.
Keep believing in what you cannot see.

Personal Reflection: Write a statement of faith based
on your understanding of God and a situation you are
experiencing.

_____

_____

_____

_____

_____

_____

Daily Prayer

God of Impossibilities,
I praise Your mighty name.

When my life is troubled and my
enemies seem too big, remind me how
great You are and that the battle is Yours,
not mine. Please help me to remember
that I just need to stand still and
trust in Your faithfulness.

Nothing is too hard for You, God.
No adversity is too great. No situation is
too difficult. It does not matter what it
looks like, feels like, or sounds like,
with You, all things are possible.

Thank You for fighting my battles.
Thank You for causing me to win.
In Jesus' name

When we wake up in the morning,
we do not know how our day will end.
Will we make it to and from our destinations?
Will our children be safe at school?
Will a person, seeking to bring harm, enter our
workplace and wreak havoc on the innocent?
Will we hear heartbreaking news, become
a victim to identity theft, fall prey to a
scammer, or contract some serious virus?

The good news is that no matter what we
encounter, our destiny is secure in Christ,
and we have a sovereign God, mighty in power,
who is faithful to help us in all our experiences.
Sometimes the outcome is not what we want,
but God can take what the enemy meant for
our ruin and turn it around for our good.

30.

Worthless Weapons

*"No weapon formed against you shall proper,
and every tongue which rises against you in
judgment you shall condemn. This is the heritage
of the servants of the LORD, and their
righteousness is from Me," says the LORD.*
Isaiah 54:17 NKJV

Prophetic Affirmations

No weapon formed against me shall prosper.
No plan of the enemy shall prevail over my life.
No attack in any form shall triumph over me.
I am more than a conqueror in Christ.

No weapon formed against me shall prosper.
No ploy to bring me down will succeed.
My righteousness is from the Lord.
I am more than a conqueror in Christ.

No weapon formed against me shall prosper.
God will work all things out for my good.
My destiny is secure in Christ.
I am more than a conqueror in Christ.

No weapon formed against me shall prosper.
No plan of the enemy shall prevail over my life.
No attack in any form shall triumph over me.
I am more than a conqueror in Christ.

Declare these affirmations over and over.
Renew your mind by what you say!

Personal Reflection: What words will you speak today to reinforce a positive mindset?

_____

_____

_____

_____

_____

_____

Daily Prayer

Almighty God and Giver of Life,
I honor your awesome name.

I do not know what will happen in
my life today, but I do know that
You will be with me, protecting me,
shielding me, and leading me
in the way that I should go.

Thank You for helping me to be spiritually
sensitive to the strategies the enemy has set
up against me, and cognizant of people and
situations that could potentially bring me harm.
Thank You that no weapon formed
against me shall prosper.
Thank You for giving me victory in You.
In Jesus' name

Every word of God proves true.
He is a shield to all who come
to him for protection.
Proverbs 30:5 NLT

Speak the Word
until you see things from a biblical perspective,
until you believe that nothing is too hard for God,
until you surrender everything to the Lord,
until you acknowledge God in everything.

Speak the Word
until you trust the mercies of God,
until you believe that God can save you,
until you honor the Lord in every situation,
until you learn to rest in what God says.

Speak the Word
until the light of day shines in your darkest hour,
until you exalt God above every problem,
until the hope of victory permeates your soul,
until you know, beyond all doubt,
that God will help you.

Help Lord, Help!

Prophetic Affirmations for Yourself

What are Prophetic Affirmations?

They are words YOU SAY that
agree with God.

They are statements YOU MAKE
that correspond with the scriptures.

When to Speak Prophetic Affirmations?

Several times a day,
in the morning,
when you go to bed,
when you feel lonely or afraid,
when you feel hopeless or discouraged,
when you need wisdom and guidance,
when you need strength and peace,
when you need counsel and comfort,
when you need deliverance,
when you need help!

Now that you know what Prophetic Affirmations are, how they work and how to apply them to your life, it is time to personalize them for yourself. I have created a worksheet for you to write your own Prophetic Affirmations. This method of writing and speaking will help you persevere through the many challenges and adversities that life brings. Keep in mind that Prophetic Affirmations are not just for troubled times. They are also a means to keep us focused on purposeful living, as well as a beautiful form of praise and thanksgiving to God.

I pray that you will continue to use this format to deepen your spiritual walk, strengthen your mind, and bring about a lasting change to the way you approach adversity.

Let's get started!

Prophetic Affirmations for Yourself

1. If you feel defeated over a situation in your life, remember that you can overcome all things with God on your side. Create a Prophetic Affirmation beginning with "I can overcome_____ because God is on my side." Repeat it over and over until you believe what you say.

   _____

   _____

   _____

   _____

2. Write three Prophetic Affirmations based on Psalm 138:8 – *"The Lord will work out His plans for my life"* and apply them to a situation you are currently experiencing.

   _____

   _____

   _____

   _____

3. Psalm 121:2 says, *"My help comes from the Lord."* Write a Prophetic Affirmation acknowledging that God is always ready to help us. "God will help me _____."

   _____

   _____

   _____

   _____

4. *"May I never forget the good things God does for me"* (Psalm 103:2). No matter what you face today, write two Prophetic Affirmations beginning with "I will remember_____."

   _____

   _____

   _____

   _____

5. Write about a challenge you are facing. Then write two Prophetic Affirmations that will help you remember that God is with you. Speak them over your life several times a day.

_____

_____

_____

_____

6. Who do you need God to be for you today – A comforter, counselor, advocate, provider, deliverer, healer, savior? In faith, write down several Prophetic Affirmations confessing who God is to you. Example: "God is my _____."

_____

_____

_____

_____

7. Write a Prophetic Affirmation that begins with "I want." Write it again beginning with "I can." Rewrite the same one beginning with "I will." Lastly, begin the statement with "I am."

_____

_____

_____

_____

8. Prophetic Affirmations are statements that align with the promises of God. Romans 8:37 says, _"We are more than conquerors through Him who loved us."_ Write three statements beginning with "I am more than a conqueror even when_____."

_____

_____

_____

_____

9. Joshua 1:9 says, *"God is with us wherever we go"*– in the courtroom, surgical unit, prison ward, workplace, school, or just at home. Acknowledge God's presence by writing and speaking a Prophetic Affirmation applicable to your life.

_____

_____

_____

_____

10. *"The righteous person may have many troubles, but the Lord delivers him from them all"* (Psalm 34:19). Think about any troubles/challenges you may have, including negative thoughts, and complete the following Prophetic Affirmation – "God will deliver me from_____."

_____

_____

_____

_____

11. Sometimes life is so hard. But even in times of adversity, God continues to bless us. Create three Prophetic Affirmations beginning with "God blesses me each day with _____."

_____

_____

_____

_____

12. Habakkuk 2:3 says, *"Write the revelation and make it plain on tablets."* If there is a specific promise or a revelation God has given you, write it down in the form of a Prophetic Affirmation and repeat it often until you have what you say.

_____

_____

_____

_____

God is a present help in trouble.
He can turn hard times into bearable ones.
He can heal our bodies and renew our minds.
He can comfort us in our weakest hour and
strengthen us to persevere. God will carry
us in His arms and hide us in the shadow
of His wings. He will blanket us with His
grace and sustain us with His mighty power.

Remind yourself often about the goodness of
God and His faithfulness to those He loves.

Use your voice to bless yourself!

Printed in the United States
by Baker & Taylor Publisher Services